HeartStorm

SIMONE HALL

HeartStorm

Heartbreak as a Catalyst for Profound
Introspection, Healing, and Personal Growth

ROSEBUD PRESS
EGG HARBOR TWP., NJ

Copyright © 2025 by Simone Hall.

All rights reserved.

No part of this publication may be reproduced, distributed, or transmitted in any form or by any means, including photocopying, recording, or other electronic or mechanical methods, without the written permission of the publisher, except in the case of brief quotations embodied in critical reviews and specific other noncommercial uses permitted by copyright law. For permission requests, write to the publisher at the email address below.

Simone Hall/Rosebud Press
ISBN 979-8-9925782-0-1

hello@simonehall.com

HeartStorm: Heartbreak as a Catalyst for Profound Introspection, Healing and Personal Growth/ Simone Hall.–1st ed.

Contents

Introduction....7

a longing....9

prelude....13

the tempest....23

the eye....37

the aftermath....45

an invitation...57

healing space....58

Acknowledgments....60

*For all the hearts that have weathered the storm,
may you always find the strength to bloom again.*

Introduction

This poetry collection is a companion for those in pain—and a roadmap for those seeking growth and self-discovery.

HeartStorm traces an intensely personal journey as an invitation to you to embrace your own storms. Page by page, you'll see that the potential for profound personal growth, healing, and renewal awaits right there within the tempest.

This book is for you, whether you're in the thick of navigating heartbreak or seeking a deeper understanding of the human experience.

HeartStorm is more than just a poetry collection; it's a testament to the power of art and self-reflection to transform us and deliver us to a calm, safe refuge.

a longing

To be soul to soul–

closer than whisper and gentle touch.

Even when you're on the other side of the world.

To be a stone's throw away and still crave your touch.

To look into your eyes and know your thoughts—

for you to mirror my actions and be aware of my thoughts too.

To know that your thoughts often drift to our entwined souls when I gaze at the moon.

To know that my heart beats to the rhythm of you;

The pulse of our bodies keeping our spirits in tune.

This is what I dream, desire, deserve.

I know that you're here, somewhere,

so patiently, I'll wait for you.

-Intimacy

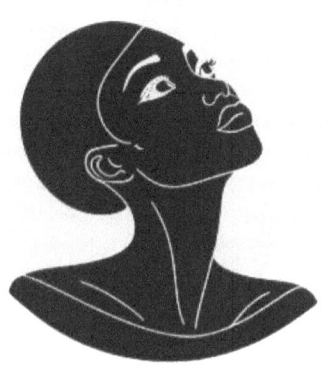

prelude

Let me tell you the story of how I accidentally fell in love. No amount of pre-date texting and chatting could have prepared me for the wave of golden warmth that washed over me the moment we laid eyes on each other for the first time. When our eyes met, I knew instantly that I was in danger. His presence took my breath away and the depth in his eyes disarmed me. The air between us was electric and warm, even though it was barely 30 degrees outside.

He approached me, hands in pocket, shoulders to ears, trying to block the frosty night air from assaulting his neck.

"Hi." he drew out slowly, a smile spreading across his face as he spread his arms wide and enfolded me in the warmest hug.

Mmmm, he smells good. Mmmm, this feels good. I thought to myself. I most definitely exhaled.

"Hi," I replied, equally enthused. I could feel myself melting as I stood there wrapped in the oddly familiar comfort of his arms. The space between his arms felt like it had been waiting for me; had been carved out, especially for me.

I gathered myself as we broke from our embrace. I could not understand what was happening to me. How could this man have had this effect on me, when we had only said hello? Yes, it had been a good minute since I had even gone on a date, but the way that my entire being responded to him solely based on a hello and a hug; I just could not make any sense of what I was feeling. We were physically meeting for the first time, but my soul recognized him right away.

As luck would have it, the restaurant where we met was about to close and so were all the surrounding restaurants, thanks to the abbreviated business hours that began during COVID.

Neither of us wanted the night to end before it even had a chance to begin; we stood in the parking lot and came up with an alternative that has easily become one of the most unintentionally intimate, romantic, and unforgettable moments of my life.

For reasons I still cannot figure out, I felt a familiar sense of comfort with him that I still feel and cannot explain. I felt so comfortable that I decided to leave my car behind and travel with him while we figured out a way to keep our evening from coming to a premature end.

"I was trying my hardest to make it down here for our original time, but that last delivery took a lot longer than I thought it would. I'm glad you still wanted to get together though; I've been looking forward to this." He said, glancing over at me to take in the expression on my face.

"Same, I've been looking forward to it too. I'm not home for much longer and I wanted to get together before I head back to Japan. Plus, the past few weeks have been so heavy with the passing of my stepfather, I needed this. So, thank you." I replied, genuinely thankful to be escaping my reality for a little while.

"I figured you could use some time away with all that you have going on right now, so I'm glad I could help you out with that. I just feel bad that I didn't realize everything would be closed by the time I got down here."

"Don't feel bad, I hadn't thought of that either. But I'm sure we'll figure something out. Honestly, I'm just happy to be out of the house."

"I just got an idea, there's one spot that I can think of that I know is always open, it's not fancy or an eat-in place, but we could do carry-out and eat in my truck. Would that be all right with you?"

"That sounds good to me. Like I said, at this point, I'm just happy to be out of the house and getting some fresh air."

After some easy conversation, we pulled up to a grubby little pizzeria in the city that didn't subscribe to the early closing hours that the other businesses had once COVID hit.

"Ay, my man. Good to see ya!" Cried out the short-order cook as we walked into the restaurant."

He and the cook exchanged a few pleasantries and laughs before he returned his attention to me.

"I come in here *a lot* after rehearsal," he said stretching his eyes open wide.

"I see that," I laughed.

We made our way back to the car with our food and drinks where we sat and talked and ate, and talked some more, and laughed. Our conversation flowed naturally from one topic to the next, no pauses, no skips – just ebb and flow, and it was refreshing. By the time we finished our meal, we were talking about our childhoods, where we grew up and how.

"We're actually not far from where I grew up, you feel like taking a ride to see it, or are you ready to go home?"

"I'm having a good time, and I'd like to see your childhood home and hear some good stories, let's go," I replied, pleasantly surprised by the way the night was unfolding.

"I was hoping you said that," he replied, a half-smile dancing across his lips. "Plus, there's a nice spot where we can park and keep the conversation going if you feel like it."

About 15 minutes later, we were circling the block looking at some older bayside apartments before he stopped in front of a particular building unit and began to recount some of his childhood memories of how he used to get into trouble for hanging outside too long with his friends. I couldn't help but take in all the expressions that subtly crossed his face as he reflected on his childhood. Before he got too lost in his memories, he returned to the present, and we made our way to the bayside to park and continued our conversation.

The moon shone brightly over the dark, cold bay. The short beach stretched out in front of us. As I gazed at the beautiful view and let myself be present in the moment, he focused on changing the music to an album that matched the vibe that we had created in our private little orb.

The music was soulful, enchanting, delicious, and added to the electricity that was steadily growing between us. We continued to talk and vibe with the music, sometimes letting the conversation drift into moments of comfortable silence.

"What are you over there thinking about?" I asked curiously.

"Honestly, how I cannot believe how dope this is. How dope *you* are. I'm really enjoying talking to you, and just how it feels to be here with you right now. I mean I expected to have a good time, but this is…different."

"I was hoping you said that and that it wasn't just me. I feel like we have known each other longer than tonight. I mean I know we text and talk on the phone, but this just feels, I don't know, like you said… different."

We sat reclined in our seats, letting the music play, and continuing the conversation as we felt necessary, our limbs somehow inched closer toward each other. At one point his arm moved flush against mine, and in that moment my body became fire from the inside out. His arm touched me, and my body lost its ever-loving mind.

What in the WORLD is going on with you, girl? I thought to myself, incredulously. *You have got to calm down, you are doing A LOT.*

While I sat there trying and failing to calm myself down, I realized that he must have felt the fire too, because he grabbed my hand and caressed it in a way that made me know that he didn't have any desire to let it go anytime soon. At that moment, I leaned into his chest and allowed my head to rest just below his chin. The second round of flames occurred as he brought his free hand to my head and began to gently play in my hair.

Defenses down, I did not pull away when we found ourselves cheek to cheek; I delighted in the warmth of his breath against my ear. I became intoxicated as we stared deeply, longingly into each other's eyes. And I gave myself over willingly when our lips met for one of the most intentional, deliberate, and seductive kisses I have ever experienced.

Not wanting the moment to end, we settled back into the warmth of each other's embrace and sat in comfortable silence while the music played. That comfortable silence stretched into a slumber that was only disrupted by his gentle snores. At my prompting, he woke up and we made our way back to my car, barely beating the sun.

"I feel like it goes without saying, but I had a really good time with you tonight," he said as we stood in an embrace while my car engine warmed.

"Me too," I replied, my response muffled by his embrace.

"No, I don't think you understand, I haven't felt like this about anyone in a long time. I feel like I'm in high school," he laughed.

"I think I do," I replied smiling up at him. "Listen, it's late and you have a bit of a drive ahead of you, let me know when you make it home."

"Okay, I'll let you know when I make it home, and I'll call you tomorrow. Well, I guess I mean later today," he replied before leaning down and giving me a goodbye kiss. "And you let me know once you make it home too."

We said our goodbyes and I floated home on cloud nine.

The night had been so unexpectedly magical that I couldn't help but replay the night's events over and over in my mind as I got myself ready for bed. The conversation, the connection, the *kiss*; there was no way I was going to be able to settle down and go to sleep. So, I did the only thing I could do at that hour, the thing that came naturally, I took out my journal and my pen, and I began to write.

the tempest

How long does it take to fall in love?

To occupy the same space and say nothing.
Occupy the same space and say everything.

To feel the intoxicatingly charged air that permeates the space between two people.

To get lost in the grit and depth of his voice.

To feel soft and womanly.

To feel effortless, natural.

To have conversations that stretch into silence.

Into touches, glances, lips meeting lips.

Touch of hand.

  Hand in hair.

    Cheek to cheek.

      Breath to ear.

Two dates. Long dates.

I am Undone. Disarmed. Beside myself.

The embodiment of reckless abandon.

There is danger in falling from so high…. Yet, I am willing to fall–*yearning* to fall.

Falling.

I hope,

  Hope.

He catches me.

-Honeydew Melon

Can we play pretend and just say that you're mine?

I know not quite yet, but I feel it will happen in time.

- an interlude

I'm being reckless with my feelings again

yearning to let him in

into all of *me*

mind

body

heart

soul

I want him to

know

me

to see, feel, understand …what lies beneath.

Venture down into the unknown depths of my essence

to find the fragile, delicate, complex core hidden behind walls erected years ago

I want to

know

him too

and to save me

from getting lost

in a sea of counterfeit love

and crooked smiles

I wonder,

can I make him

let me?

-Reckless

I felt…

Wanted.

Desired.

Sought after.

Precious.

Sexy.

Interesting.

Respected.

Understood.

Comfortable.

Safe.

Certain.

Confident.

Joyful.

Cared for.

Considered.

I feel...

Cast aside.

Conquered.

Less than.

Used.

Obsolete.

Objectified.

Confused.

Angry.

Disappointed.

Tricked.

Hoodwinked.

Duped.

Ashamed.

Foolish.

Dismissed.

Drawbridge up. Fortress guarded. Treasure buried. Dragon protected. Please leave.

I am not interested.

I am not in distress.

I do not need saving.

I reject your kiss.

-In a Moment

Were you reckless with my heart,
knowing what it had just survived?
Or did you think I was a big girl that knew how
to compartmentalize?
Looking in your eyes, I could have sworn that
you knew—
the Love growing within my heart, only for you.
When we were together, I felt your Love too—
wrapping my heart in the sweetest embrace
before abruptly rushing out of the door in haste.

-Whiplash

I was so close…
I thought that I had
found my forever in you
I know what I saw
I know how I felt then
I know how I feel now
I know how you looked at me then
I *feel* how you look at me now
Your love slipped right through my fingertips
At least it feels that way
There is true desire, but I see a shadow of
something I can't name—
What is keeping you from me?
Memories of you burn on my heart—
Painfully holding vigil for you
You are my greatest love
You are my greatest heartbreak
Sometimes I feel like there is no way I'll recover
from you
It shatters my Heart to think that you don't feel
the same way that I do
To know you are the one thing that I genuinely
desire and cannot have
I don't think I've known hurt like this before
I see you in everything I do
I can't believe that you can't feel how intensely
and often I think about you,
Pray for you,
Send my love to you

And the pain that I feel knowing that you aren't
feeling the same way about me
This rejection has rubbed my heart raw
I've made myself a fool for you

I wonder if you know how I'm hurting for you or
if you would even care if you did?
My third eye is blind when it comes to you…
Or am I choosing not to see the obvious?

-We Were So Close

You came
          and
                h u n g r i l y
                    ate
                        from my tree
devouring
                    some
              of the
    sweetest
              parts
                of
                  me
You became
      a d d i c t e d

              to the
                most
    delicious
              fruit
I confused
      your
        a d d i c t i o n
                  for a genuine
              desire
            to understand
              my
            roots.

-Grizzly

the eye

I must believe that this is the salve.
Right now–
this time,
this moment,
this season.
This is my healing,
my lesson,
my growth.
Nothing else would be a suitable explanation for
this hole,
this pit,
this painful cavity.
I must Believe,
Feel,
Know…
I must be certain that this leads to
Something.
Something *more*
Something *greater*,
Something *higher*.
The pain is too great for it all to have been for
naught.
I choose to Trust,
Believe,
Feel,
Know,
That this severance was necessary for reasons.
Reasons that encapsulate my entirety—

Reasons that catapult me into moving in flow
with my purpose.
The pain is
Too deep,
Too long lasting,
Too far reaching—
To be purposeless.

Because my love is too big to be ignored—
Rejected,
Cast aside so easily…

Isn't it?

-Alchemy

My biggest mistake was walking through this world
with an open heart.
Thinking—mistakenly, foolishly, innocently—
that the hearts I met along the way would be like mine.
Feel like mine.
See like mine.
Believe like mine.
Operate like mine.
Care like mine.
Love like mine.
Know—like mine.
I'm ashamed how long it's taken me to grab hold of the painful truth.
My naivete,
My optimism,
My ignorance,
My hope?
My *need* to believe—
Left my heart open; vulnerable.

My heart has been
Pricked,
Stabbed,
Squeezed,
Squished,
Stolen,

Broken,
Battered,
Bruised,
Deceived,
Rejected,
Forgotten,
Manipulated,
Abandoned,

Forced into seclusion—
Shelter.
A place of protection,
Refuge,
Recluse,
Invisibility,
Absence,
Rest,
Recuperation,
Sorting,
Healing,
Restructuring.
Where I was made to meet myself in my entirety.
In my Wholeness.
In my Shadows and
In my Light.
Understand my culpability in creating my own emotional ruins.
make peace with it and rebuild—
from the ground up, with hard earned wisdom.

Under new management and watchful eye.

"Yield. Be Watchful, Mindful, Intentional,
Present.
Apply what you've learned, and protect your
heart, babe."
My Higher Self vibrates, knowingly with hopeful
anticipation of the future.

-Seasons

I am purple–
deep, rich, Divine.
I am royalty–
majesty, magic, and mysticism
all rolled into one.
I am the hue that demands deep admiration
and respect.
I am held in high regard by all those who behold
the beauty
of my visage.

-Crown

the aftermath

For thirty years I've kept my heartache folded up
tightly
like the most intricate origami—
there is beauty in the pain of unfurling.

-Origami

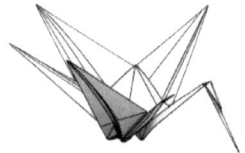

I feel untethered, like I'm drifting away
the idea of "work" feels like an abstract concept—
compared to my Destination.
I don't know its exact location—
but I'm coming to know how it's supposed to feel—
as it comes to me in the briefest of glimmers.

I feel untethered, like I'm drifting away
I can't tell if I'm floating or sinking.
Until the warmth of sunshine on my face reminds me—
I inhale the Instruction to release the tension of uncertainty.
I exhale the Divine understanding that it is my time
to finally let go
and float.

-Float

My truth feels most safe
when my tears are honored —
given space
Not rushed to be collected, dried, or put away
It feels most safe when it isn't being judged
or corrected,
or rewrapped in more presentable packaging
so it is more palatable
It feels most safe
when I can speak openly and freely without
intentional crafting of delivery
My truth feels most safe where it is welcome,
pondered—
met with genuine probing questions that crave
understanding on a deeper level
My truth feels most safe when it is regarded with
the most tender of intentions and gentle care

-Altar

What are these tears springing from my heart?
It feels like healing water.

-Release

I found Joy today
in the truth
of sharing my heart.

She was so quiet,
I almost missed her.

-Unassuming

Joy found me
  when I found the truth.

Joy found me
  when I found honesty.

Joy found me
  when I found my voice.

Joy found me
  when I found myself.

Joy has found me at long last.

-HeartSong

Becoming myself
feels like
the most glorious
Unfolding.

It feels like
the discovery of the most
Precious Gem;
a gem no one
has yet had the privilege to
discover
or
possess.

-Authenticity

Love—

a tiny, determined seedling
emerging
triumphantly
from the soil of my heart.

-Restored

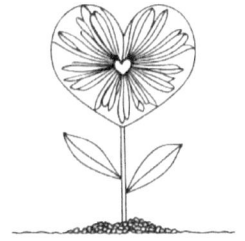

a little something for you, dear reader...

Take a moment to listen to the playlist I put together while writing this book—it's a musical reflection of my heart space throughout my healing process.

Be sure to visit **simonehall.com** for links to my Substack space and various creative goodies to come.

an invitation

Heartbreak, while undeniably painful, is a catalyst for introspection, healing, and growth. Heartbreak forced me to go on a journey to find pain points far beneath the surface, and reckon with long-buried emotions and experiences. Along the way, writing emerged as a powerful healing tool. It allowed me to articulate complex emotions, providing a safe space for self-acceptance and reflection. Each word I penned helped me explore vulnerabilities, identify relationship patterns, and clarify my needs. This cathartic release transformed sorrow into tangible thoughts I could acknowledge and release. Over time, my writing documented not just pain, but also personal growth, and it helped me celebrate small victories.

I invite you to embark on a similar journey — embrace your own heartbreak, whatever type it may be, and use writing to navigate your emotions. You may find that through putting pen to paper, you unearth insights leading to profound personal growth and healing.

healing space

A space for you to begin your own healing journey…

_____

_____

_____

_____

_____

_____

_____

_____

_____

_____

_____

_____

_____

Acknowledgements

Thank you to my family and friends for loving, supporting, and encouraging me through my creative process and cheering me on as I saw this project through to completion.

Thank you, Alex Elle and Kemi Nekvapil, for encouraging me to "write the book," and "tell my story," I am forever grateful for your encouragement.

Thank you, Elle, for the creation of the Brave Writer's Group, such a nurturing creative space that I look forward to joining every other Sunday afternoon.

Thank you, Rumi, for seeing a need and filling it with the creation of the Your Tiny Beautiful Book community.

Thank you to the YTBB community members: Dave, Hana, Renee, and Sabah, you'll never know how helpful I found the discussions in the group chat.

Thank you, Renee, for your (multiple) review(s) of my manuscript and helping me to present my art in the best way possible.

And thank you, dear reader, for taking the time to read from the pages of my heart.

♡

Coming soon...

from, *BirdSong*

We can't predict the future, or the course of events that will take place in our lives; at times being rerouted altogether. Every now and then, if we are quiet enough and allow not only our ears to hear, but our spirits too, we are given hints, clues, and glimpses of what is to come. I clearly recall the exact moment I became aware that the Wheel of Fortune was set to turn for me, although I had no idea how soon that moment would come or how profoundly it would impact the trajectory of my life.

It was in the wee hours of a long, cold night in February while nestled in the cozy warmth of my bed, that I was awoken from a deep slumber with a start. It was 2:22 am when my eyes flew open and scanned the moonlit corners of my bedroom, searching in vain for the culprit that awakened me at the ungodly hour. Within moments, I heard a voice that was not my own, speak calmly and deliberately to my startled spirit, *"You're going to drink and smoke yourself to death."* It wasn't said angrily; there was no trace of judgment or condemnation, simply a statement of fact. A fact that I knew in my core to be true.

As I lay there in the dark silence, ruminating on the message that was delivered to me at that oddly specific time, my mind set itself on a task that kept me awake until the sounding of my alarm at 5:30 am. Reflecting on the past, reviewing my present-day habits, and wondering about the future. My mind was flooded with thoughts; I couldn't help wondering how my life would unfold if I did nothing, if I simply ignored the warning and continued heading down the path I was on. Surely, the voice didn't mean actual death, did it? Of course it did, I had an inner knowing that I couldn't shake. With that thought, I put together a slapdash plan that would help pull me out of the poor habits I had formed.

I thought to myself, "Limit the wine, limit the herbal refreshments, take walks. I'll be fine, I just need these things to help me cope right now. I'll get it together."

"You're going to drink and smoke yourself to death." That message stayed with me throughout the day, followed me to bed that evening, permeated my dreams, and arose with

me the next morning. I couldn't let it go, and I knew it was the truth.

About the Author

Simone Hall is an author based in New Jersey, where she weaves together poetry, prose, and delightful musings that capture the heart. With her little red dog, Rosie Valentine, by her side, Simone finds inspiration in the everyday magic of life. When she's not writing, you can find her curled up with a good book or sharing laughter over a glass of red wine with cherished friends. With a warm and inviting style, Simone aims to enchant readers with her words, proving that storytelling can be both a joyful escape and a heartfelt connection. *HeartStorm* is her first book. You can find more of Simone's writing at simonehall.com

www.ingramcontent.com/pod-product-compliance
Lightning Source LLC
LaVergne TN
LVHW041225080526
838199LV00083B/3347